AN ODE
TO THE FIVE ELEMENTS I BECAME THIS YEAR

By Melissa Felson

Printed in the United States of America
First Printing, 2021
ISBN 978-1-949321-24-1

All writings within this book belong to the author.
Cover Art Image by: Steven Felson
Cover Design by: Austie M. Baird
Illustrations by: Steven Felson

A.B.Baird Publishing
66548 Highway 203
La Grande OR, 97850
USA
www.abbairdpublishing.com

DEDICATION

This book is dedicated

to every family member, friend and imagined foe

who has been a part of my journey.

I will be

forever grateful

for the lessons they have taught me

and the way they have

shaped me into

who I am.

AN ODE TO THE FIVE ELEMENTS I BECAME THIS YEAR

    I.   sand:

when the waves came,
          no one knew what would become of you

                              your structure,
                    your solidity,
              crumbled into granular
          dust, scattered upon the foam
and floated off into the unknown

thank you
          for your
                    fluidity

II.   mud:

for some time, there
        you were quite sloppy

                        soggy mess drenched in wet,
                thick and branded with the
            imprint of someone else's boot
but, in time, you allowed yourself
to bake into something new, something solid

thank you
        for your
                longevity

III. stone:

hard and cold
        became your battle cry

                        you willed yourself into a wall,
                    imagined yourself upright
                until your legs became pillars
            and you were no longer
just bits of rock on a cold hard ground

thank you
        for your
                strength

Melissa Felson

IV.   brick:

in time, you shed your pallid slab
        and began your reconstruction

                        no longer like a prison, gray
                    and sheathed in lengths of wire;
                nor frail enough to be blown down
        by wolves with fickle ways;
with wiser hands you built yourself anew

thank you
        for your
                ingenuity

V.   clay

you've learned
          that you are made for molding

                              not for drowning in a fickle wave;
                              not as sludge beneath another's weight;
                    not for shutting out the chance of threat;
          or even standing firm against the winds;
you are meant to grow and shift and change

so
thank you
          for your
                    bravery

CONTENTS

SAND

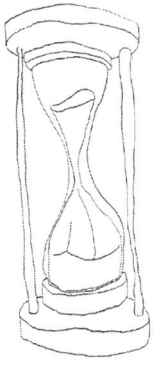

Stop setting up camp in sandcastles.

Your heart could never belong

somewhere so easily dismantled.

DIVINATIONS

I have a memory
of a little girl,
alone on a bedroom carpet,
trying to control her
spinning-top world
with a Magic-8 Ball.

It will take her
the rest of her life
to realize
that she can't.

Melissa Felson

ASSAULT

.

we stand among a field of sunlit flowers
when cool breeze turns to thrashing wind;
the air, a tinge of salt
certain of our fate, a lie forlorn
the calm before the fatal storm
awaiting the assault

slowly but surely the waves erode the sand;
I pause and take a longing glance
as the castle walls come down
the captain goes down with his ill-fated ship –
I catch a glimpse as you abandon ship
while, here, I slowly drown

WHEN THE BOY SAYS HE LOVES ME
after Bianca Phipps "When the Boy Says He Loves My Body"

when the boy says he loves me
but his hands are wrapped around his own body
I settle for pretending I am his body

when the boy says he loves me
and his eyes are shut tight like curtained mirrors
I wonder if he ever takes those curtains down
and if he does, who does he see?

when the boy says he loves me,
I believe him

FIXING YOU

Fixing
you is the hardest thing
I've ever
never done.

Loving you
is
everything and
nothing all
in one.

Needing
you
is
trudging
through
the
mud
on solid ground.

But fixing you -
oh, fixing you -
is a scream without the sound.

BUT YOU DIDN'T

When I came to
our apartment
to pick my things up (off the floor),
also, to leave the keys on the counter:
I laid in
your bed,
I cried into
your pillow,
and I hoped
that you would notice it…

BROKEN

Broken is a thing I've met before.
In the lines of his tattoo that I used to trace,
In the gap between his teeth
just small enough to be sweet,
In the playfulness of his bright blue eyes
and his dusty blonde cropped hair.
But never.
Did I think.
We'd meet again.
In you.

Broken is a knife whose blade I've felt
and lived to tell the tale.

Broken is a monster
in whose snarling face I've laughed.

Broken is a villain I'd thought I'd slain, at last, in you.

Good thing I kept my sword.

EVER EMPTYING CHAIRS

Have you ever seen
  an empty chair
     so pregnant
      with the weight of the past,

    the way it
    sits heavy
    on your heart,

   the way it creaks
   in your chest

     to see it
      unoccupied,

     to see it
      wanting,

    to see
    the way it
    holds
      so
        little
    and yet
    so much?

Have you ever noticed
how the empty chairs
multiply?

How
each time you look
they are
less
and
less full

more
and
more
full of hurt?

How they are
a garden
backwards growing
toward barren?

An Ode: Sand

How they are
memories
f
a
d
i
n
g
into the fabric?

Have you ever noticed
how much
life
can resemble
a room
of ever
emptying
chairs?

THE PLACES I LOVED HIM

The inner folds of his ears
The undersides of his palms
The space between his toes
The arches of his feet

The whites of his eyes
The pores of his skin
The cavity of his skull
The convolutions of his brain

These are The Places I Loved Him
These, too, are The Places I Lost Him

MAYBE:

How,
when you first heard the faint alarms
in the midst of our Saturday morning sunlight,
did you not stop to warn me?

I might have found the fire with you:
Check the cabinets!
      under the sinks!
           in the closets!
                under the bed!

Maybe we would have found it
together,
there in the folds of our darkest thoughts
in your soul, in mine.

Maybe (and I know this is only a maybe)
we *could* have extinguished it.

Held on for dear life in the scorching heat:
The walls melting around us,
their plaster and paint
seeping into the cracks in our armor
as we embraced, anchors in the center;
joint phoenixes finding strength in the struggle.

Maybe then we wouldn't have ended up here:
Separate sides of a bed we shared,
the ashes of our love settling around us, *a soft rain,*
drenching us in everything unspoken
everything
                    unsearched

                              and untouched...

Maybe:
we'll never know.

SWALLOW

I scream into notebook pages

because you are not here

and because, if you were,

I would just swallow it all anyway.

FALLEN

I dropped my secrets in the sea
They sunk to the ocean floor like bodies
Striving for sustenance

They baked in the sun until the yeast rose
And the oven rang

But I, I shriveled in the Atlantic winds
Turned inside out
I positioned scabs to cover my wounds

But the northern gale ripped them away
And so,
Plagued with the salty aftertaste of catastrophe
My ship and I rode quietly away
Hopeful ears pricked for bubbles whispering closure
Bubbles from the ocean floor
Bubbles which never rise

TOFURKEY

When I think of how you broke my heart,
I remember:
myself
and a package of Tofurkey.

It had been two months
since you sent me staggering
from our apartment on the water,
where sun and open air swirled
through our kitchen windows
and I swayed – humming to myself, to colgate walls and
an emerald countertop – as I prepared tomorrow's lunch.

And when I think of how you broke my heart
I remember:
the resolve with which I made that sandwich.

How it represented everything you had taken from me
and everything I would not let you take.
How I stormed through the grocery store entrance, teeth gritted,
foraging for ingredients that I had once tucked tenderly
in our reusable shopping bags.
Every step, every clink,
every turn I took to reach my parents' home,
a refusal to allow you to stop me.

And when I think of how you broke my heart
I remember:
myself and a package of Tofurkey
in my parents' kitchen,
deep chestnut accents harsh against faux bricks,
darkened almost black.

And I remember, like it was yesterday,
the sudden, bursting, searing pang in my chest
as I opened the soft cardboard,
revealing cold cuts caught in shrink-wrapped plastic
and I,
on impulse,
reached for the familiar black-rimmed scissors that sit
so rightly, so well-placed,
beside an open window looking out to the sea.

A CEASELESS STORM

I purchased a plane ticket the night you left
hoping to outrun the capsizing of my heart
only to find
that it -
and you -
remain.

I AM SO MUCH

I am so much.

I am a writer,
A reader,
My parent's shining glory.
A teacher to my students
And the best damn big sister you've ever met.

I am a singer
And a poet,
And I have all the courage and conviction
Of a woman.

So why,
When I lay my head down on my pillow at night,
In a room that is all mine,
Do you invade the dreams meant only for my eyes?

And why is it that,
In my mind,
I am somehow nothing
Merely because I don't call you mine?

IF I COULD

If I could,
I would paint myself
onto the insides
of your eyelids.

Perhaps then
you might dream of me
as much as I
dream of you.

Then again,
I am not such a masterpiece.

EMBERS

How horrifying
to covet
the flames
of resilience;
then, to find
in the folds of your soul,
only embers.

MUD

*weighted blanket / the world stops
spinning for a moment / until I wake*

Melissa Felson

A CARICATURE OF ME, BY YOU

sometimes in my dreams (nightmares, really)
I see myself as I imagine you might see me

insecure little girl begging for attention
standing in corners, unworthy of mention

damaged goods harboring too much emotion
never fulfilled by her need for devotion

I am dying to believe in misinterpretation,
that the caricatures we draw of each other are false approximations

so as I fall asleep, I silently repeat
that your image bears no resemblance of me

but still I wake up from these nightmares in gasps
clawing at my face like this caricature's no mask

PRESENT, FUTURE, PAST

I can't seem to remember to put you in past tenses
what with all of our hopes for the future and hence, as
time flies by, you are a constant reminder
of what could and should, yet never will be.
I'm ashamed of my tears, but most of all me.

Somewhere in my being, there's a trace of a feeling
that the situation at hand was earlier planned.
It's a nightmare I just can't relieve myself of.
Yet in some inner crevice, a shred of hope waits
for me to at last awake.

The rest of my body knows that this theory
is merely a foolish excuse
for me to remain in this unhealthy state,
seeing you in my future though the present tells true;
You are a part of my past, you are out of my grasp,
you're a memory long overused.

MY PAST LOVERS, REPEATING

my past lovers are silhouettes against the backdrop of my loneliness
solitude spinning spells to raise them from the dirt
solemn, I watch them rise once more
unwelcome ghosts, returning

one by one, they pass before me
all scowling eyes and downturned mouths
carrying complaints in the cavities of their open chests
a deathless remonstration

right arms reach, fingers folding toward palm
coaxing regret and remorse from my throat

and again,
the air becomes heavy with old heartbreak

and again,
the shrouded figures chant their hushed and hateful hexes

repeating, repeating
well-worn sins and wrong-doings

repeating, repeating
the reasons I am alone

MY LOVE LANGUAGE MUST BE
after Zane Frederick - @zanefrederickwrites

swallowing / swallowing bitter
swallowing deep / conversations at midnight
at midnight / deep
craters hollowing / my bones
for you / swallowing
whatever you'll give me / bitter
or sweet / conversations at midnight
hollowing me / deep
and you / swallowing sweet
while I / am hollowing deep
swallowing / craters
craters / at midnight
swallowing / bitter
swallowing / deep
swallowing / me

REPLAYING YOU

found recordings of us writing music last night

I think I'll be replaying you

for the rest of my life

PIECES

You arrive in pieces…

books on a mahogany table / plants hanging / a long nap under a white comforter on a Sunday afternoon / freckled skin / eyes closed on a couch / breathing in the notes of your guitar / boots in rising water and laughter pealing from an open window / the feeling of home / that was less about walls / and more about warmth / a library / a planetarium / something about a park and talking to strangers / something about a letter written like a code /

                                something about a butterfly

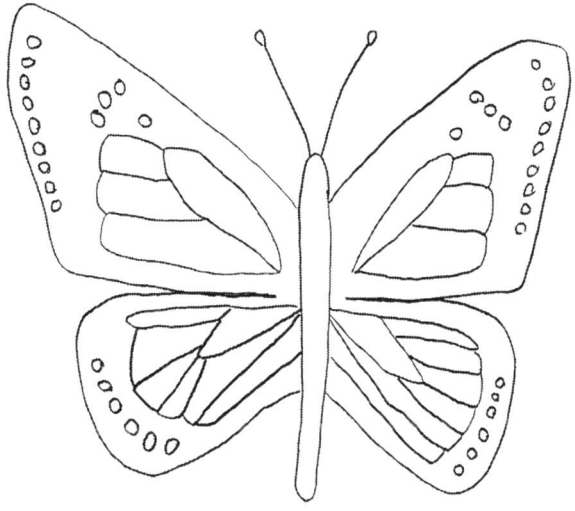

LIKE A REACHING FOR YOU

Today the universe deposited me here,
on the steps of the New York Public Library,
with the same serendipitous steps that once walked me into you.

I want to write a poem about the moments we spent here:
A snapshot in time on a sunny afternoon.

I feel compelled to,
like the very air of New York City
gathered me up
and dropped me gently and alone
on this balmy night,
whispering thematic suggestions
of love and loss,
confronted with an opportunity
for perfect acceptance,
for this event of letting go,
for this moment of moving on.

I want to write a poem
but I can't find a single word
that won't come out
like a reaching for you,

like I'm beseeching you
to imagine me:
Sitting here on these steps
mourning what we had

when every word I write
begs you
to mourn it too.

I HAVE TAKEN TO READING POETRY

It has been 8 months since I last read a novel.
I have taken to reading poetry instead.

Manageable,
Bite-sized pieces of prose;
Pointed
but somehow,
smooth enough stones to swallow –
Unlike
those bricks on the
Barnes and Noble shelves;
Those tomes
of text that feel
like heavy tombs in my hands.

I finger their spines wistfully in
remembrance of lighter days:
Bright, blazing afternoons
in the small patch of backyard we called our own,
where I stole glances at your
caramel-stained lips
collecting a kissable, salty condensation
that arrested my concentration.
Your aftertaste lingered in every word I tried to read.

These days, though, are distinctly spineless.

I have settled for the thin
backbones of chapbooks and
the occasional anthology

the way I settle for leaning
across an empty void
to quit the light
on my single bedside table.

Perhaps, one day,
stories won't taste of salted caramel and sunshine.

Perhaps, one day,
my concentration will hold long enough
to entertain happy endings again.

Until then, I have taken to reading poetry.

A CONFESSION

I read each of my poems
imagining I am you
reading each of my poems.

WALL OF TEARS

So spare me all your hopeless lies
They're growing far too stale
Too many chances have you stole
And every time, you fail

Spare me all those promises
That never seem fulfilled
A wall of tears I stand behind
A wall that you helped build

I DON'T UNDERSTAND BOXING

"I don't understand boxing,"
my friend offers from the backseat,
a passing comment to help pass the time.

And instantly,
I want to tell her about the time you and I sat
at a hotel bar in New York City;
when we wore pajamas
just because the idea made us laugh
and watched boxing matches on the little bar TVs
because it was all they would play.

I want to tell her that
I didn't get it either

but
that I remember
how your eyes danced
in the glow of those dim amber lights
as you tried to explain why
I should keep an open mind;

and how,
by the end of the night,
we were studying uppercuts and kicks
like a pair of anthropologists,
our heads tilted at the same angle
in an easy, familiar unison.

I want to tell her that,
whether it was the way you belly laughed when I shouted at the
screens
or how your hand felt so right on my thigh that night,
I could have spent
the rest of eternity
watching boxing
in a bar in New York City;
and how
I'd do anything
to go back there again.

I want to say all of this,
but I don't want to bring down the mood.
So all I say is "Me neither."

DEAFENING SILENCE

I asked my friend to warn me
when it became played out.

To let me know
when I'd become the girl
who'd said your name too many times for it to be acceptable.

She said she would,
but I didn't need her warning.

I could sense it.

The moment when my heartbreak
was no longer comfortable for them to hear

saw the anxious, awkward shimmer in the air

heard their shriveling breath suck back into their lungs
when I mentioned you, once again.

So instead, I just let your name sink into my tongue,
carve itself into the marrow in my bones
let it settle at the very center of my skull
and resigned myself to its incessant screaming
deafening, though I am silent.

HOW TO LOVE SOMEONE

I think
I have forgotten
how to love someone.

Or maybe
I never knew
how to love
in the first place.

NOVEMBER, BE GENTLE ON ME

November, be gentle on me.
The Autumn has rubbed me raw.
Her falling leaves, like razor blades,
have sliced me clean to ribbons.

I can't recall the last time I saw the sun
peek out of this gunmetal sky
or walked with anything but biting cold
nipping hungry at my heels.

November, I know you are famous for your
whipping wintry winds and your
subtle frost surprise across the early morning windshield.
And I would never want to step on your toes.
You are in charge here, after all.

But, I beg you November, be gentle on me.
It is only Autumn,
and already I am not sure
how much more winter I can take.

YOU ATE ME FOR BREAKFAST

the dark corners of your mind
spill

black-blue ink
on cream satin dress

bursted blackberries
juice dripping
sweet tragedy

the outline of which
tears on fabric
tarnished

black liquor varnish
on pulpwood
digested

you ate me for breakfast
I'm screaming
you ate me for breakfast

I TRIED TO STOP WRITING ABOUT YOU

I tried to stop writing about you
I swear I did

but, you see,
when I stopped writing about you,
nothing else came out.

think weeks of
vacant, empty

think yawning abyss
and endless desert

as if I am solely composed
of you and memories of you

as if the column of my body,
once held aloft
by the breath that you blew through my lips,
is now
deflated

as if my every atom
vibrates
at the frequency
of a muted C string on your guitar

you see, I tried to stop writing about you
I swear I did

but it seems you are the only poem I've got left

so forgive me for writing still

WHAT IF HEARTACHE WAS A SWEATER

what if heartache was a sweater
you could keep in the back of your closet?
choose to let it collect dust
or parade around like it's always in fashion?

would you check the pockets daily
for bits of paper and scraps of the past?
or fold the fabric neatly
and get on with your damn life?

slip the sleeves off one by one
and store it gently for safekeeping?
or pull it out every so often
to check that it still fits?

what if heartache was a sweater
we could choose to keep or toss?

if heartache was a choice,
would you need its warmth or toss it off?

BLAME IT ON THE WHISKEY

I could blame it on the whiskey but
he was really just
cold chains and a cruel cheek anyway.

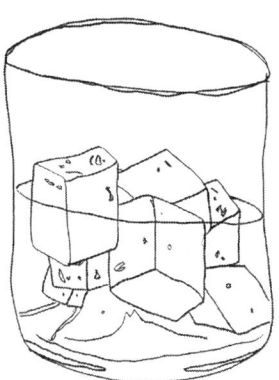

BREAKING THE HABIT

Last night,
I missed
your whiskey eyes,
missed drowning
in their
darkness,
missed sipping
on their
shrewd, smooth
single-malt sadness.

Last night,
I grabbed a glass
and thought
to pour
a double.

But then
I remembered
how you burned
on the way down,
remembered
the way you stung
to swallow,
remembered
the cheap
one-shot
wickedness
of you.

Last night,
I put down the glass.

Tucked it in the back
of the cabinet,
behind the teacups
and the coffee mugs,
and reminded myself:

some habits
are better
left
broken.

An Ode: Mud

DEPRESSION HAS BECOME A SQUATTER IN MY HOUSE

Depression stumbles through my front door
and I welcome her
with a sleeve of chocolate chip cookies
and the password to my Netflix account.

I invite Depression into my bedroom.
I know I shouldn't move this quickly,
but it just feels so right
and I was never great at resisting temptation anyway.

Depression falls into my bed and makes herself at home.
She forgets to turn the light off.
So we sleep with pillows over our heads
because the light switch is all the way on the other side of the room.

When my friends want to go to dinner,
Depression tells me she doesn't feel like going out.
So, instead, we stay home and tell ghost stories:

She tells me the one
about the girl
in a haunted house with many hallways.
From the windows, the girl sees a beautiful orchard
growing promise on its stems as bright as any apple.

But,
in Depression's version,
the girl never finds the exit sign.
Depression has become a squatter in my house.
She is a shitty boyfriend you don't know how to end things with;
An irritating aunt who has overstayed her welcome;
An overzealous friend who eats you out of house and home.

I tell her it is time for her to go.
I tell her there isn't room in here enough for the two of us.
Isn't air enough in here for both of us to breathe.
And, for the first time in a long time,
I find the exit sign.

HOW TO LEARN TO BE ANGRY

first layer of guilt / dig
warning: it will be solid
apply pressure / push
stand on the socket, if you must

break ground / breathe it in
resist the urge to vomit
(it won't smell like roses)
pull it into your nostrils, if you can stand it

keep digging / second layer
the guilt that comes
just from breathing
this one will be worse

water main break
rupture / release
let it flood the streets
submerge you, if it has to

because if you don't,
it will anyway

STONE

She stands
and stalks out the door

each step,
a sharp tack
and a swell of pride.

A BURIED SCREAM

There is a scream
buried
so far down
in my body
that you would need
to cast
a fish hook
into the bowl of my belly
to scoop it out of me.

No one
has ever seen it,
this
Loch Ness
monster
of my soul.

But it is
always there,
vibrating and
echoing
down hallways of broken veins,
churning and
smashing
into the vaulted ceilings of my skull.

No,
no one
has ever seen it,
but
believe me –
it is always there.

EVICTION

This isn't a poem;
This is an eviction notice.

A formal, type-print, size 12, white page notice.

Tacked onto a corner of my brain,
Copies pasted sloppily on my
Lips, hands, eyes, ears and heart

For posterity

Imploring you
Compelling you
Beseeching you, commanding you, demanding you

Get. Out.

Melissa Felson

MIDNIGHT SNACK

Is that king-sized bed swallowing you whole yet?
or are you still filling it with sluts,
eating out of the palm of your hand?

Are you still munching on your little midnight snacks?
or have you realized they'll never have
the substance to satisfy like I did?

(H)EX

I hope the loneliness eats you up;
A slow creep, imperceptible at the start.

An insidious black moss
beginning beneath the soles of your feet.

You'll prance around on it, stupidly,
careless in your unaffected,
invincible way.

Even when the rotting mass
wraps around your ankles like shackles,
you'll smile dumbly
at your clear complexion in the mirror.

You'll continue that way
as the loneliness snakes
through your stomach,

sometimes causing you to pause
at a sick, sucking sensation
in your gut.

But you'll go on,
shaking your heard
like a stubborn child
unwilling to face
the consequences of his selfish actions.

Until one morning,
you'll wake to find

your bright, playful eyes
(so unburdened by tears)

and your full, pink lips
(pressed careless on the bodies you flung them upon)

clouded
consumed

shrouded
entombed

in a sore, oozing mask of black
in unmistakable, unavoidable
loneliness.

I USED TO LIVE LIKE

I used to live like:
Fiddle with the faucet
till my hot and cold
are perfectly pleasing.

Muted
Measured
Lukewarm

Now I live like:
If you can't take my heat
get out of my damn shower.

EAT THE KEY

I will not be
the good woman
you crawl back to.

When you close this box,
make damn sure you are ready
to lock it up
and eat the key.

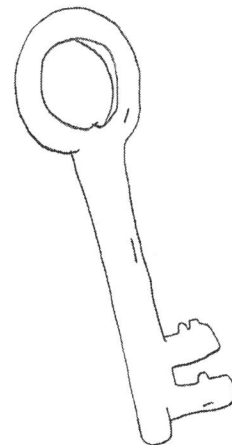

GILDED HEARTBREAK

you said that mine was a gilded heartbreak
a magic-trick mourning

my sadness was just sleight of hand

you called it
inkblot experiment heartbreak
like if you tilt your head just right
maybe the breaking never happened

you said
I seemed happier
without you

I thought you were smarter than this

didn't you know
that squinting your eyes against sunlight
is just Morse code for
it's dark in here?

and didn't you know
that a sunny glow
is just a trick mirror for shame?

and haven't you heard
that fitting better in your jeans
just means food doesn't taste like it used to?

you could say you were blinded by my silver linings

but maybe it was just easier
to picture my smile
while you slit my throat

BULLSHIT

And in the end
your pride was too large a stone to swallow.
The outline of your ego,
drawn too dark around your edges
in self-protection.

The easy way out
wrapped itself like a ribbon
around your most vulnerable parts,
tempting
coiled snake
constricting
any chance we had to make it.

You sought solace in some saccharine substance
and call it sweetness,
crowned yourself a prince
and feigned a happy ending.

But I call bullshit on any sappy crap you write.
We both know you were built for more than this.

SORRY SENRYU

For such an asshole,
you're pretty unforgiving.
You should be sorry.

SPINELESS

How does it feel to be afraid of your own shadow?

To be so unable to face your truths

you embed them in your back?

Trying to shake them off,

you bend, this way and that,

stretching yourself taut until you snap.

Trying to remove reality

like it's a thorn in your side,

but it only sinks deeper

until you are more scared than spine

- until you are practically

s

p

i

n

e

l

e

s

s.

THE THINGS THAT I MISS AND THOSE THAT I DON'T

I miss having a dishwasher.
I miss the foggy bay from our window.
I miss your cool limbs against my warm skin.

I don't miss your sister.
I don't miss your silence.
I don't miss never knowing what you were thinking.
I don't miss never feeling like I was enough to hold your gaze.

I guess what I'm saying is:
I miss not being disappointed in you,
But I don't miss being disappointed in me.

THINGS I CAN'T WAIT FOR

- a white dress on the floor of a hotel suite

    - decorating my first
    home for the holidays

- tiny feet on the kitchen tile

    - *you to be a tiny fucking*
    blip on the radar that
    is my past

WHO DO I THINK I AM?

you might be thinking:
who do I think I am?

I, with my pointed words
all thorn and no rose
all bark and all bite

what right do I have
to complain of injury
with broken brambles at my feet?

I, who would cast stones
as I stand atop jagged glass?

I, who would catalog your sins
with knees that beg for confession?

and to that I say,
aye

yet I am not the one
who feigns a diadem upon their head

who materializes wings
with which to claim a higher ground

I am neither saint nor savior

I, without honor,
without esteem,
without any pedestal upon which to perch

I do not think myself your better,
every move I make
infused
with humility and apology

but oh, how telling
that yours
still are not

SUNSHINE GIRL

By the end, I swear
you looked straight through me;
Monochrome me,
gray wisp, whisper
of what I once was
to you.

So long, I cried
that I didn't hold your eyes -
Thought I'd paled, lost my color,
failed
to be the sunshine girl
that I once was
to you.

Melissa Felson

But now, I know
it wasn't I who lost my bright
but you
who lost your sight -
color-blinded
by your own graying mind
and that I
am just as bright,
that my
job was not to hold your eyes
but just to be

and I
will always be
that sunshine girl
that I once was
to you.

YOU ARE AN EMPTY HEAT

you are an empty heat

a burning sensation in the throat
who wishes himself a fire

a shallow substance, leaking
puddle impersonating ocean
draining

you are
hollow bones
and marrow, sucked dry

you are a phantom limb
and painted smile

you are tiny paper hearts in my palm
that I whisper into the wind,

breathing my boundaries into life –
as I refuse
to let you settle into my skin;

to crawl through my veins,
to hollow out my bones
and paint yourself across my smile

because,
tempting
as your masquerade may be

your empty heat
will never be enough
to warm me

REASONS NOT TO LOVE A POET
after Sam Thomas - @reservoirsummer

   1.   You're not ready.

You haven't met your feelings yet
         and to see us
  s h a k i n g   h a n d s
        with ours
        makes your
lilly-   livered   boots   quake

              2.   You're not ready.

                 Truths are
       s l i t h e r i n g   s n a k e s,
              their bejeweled bodies
                  hidden
           behind many rocks.

        When we hold them up to the light,
        you will run.

3.   You're not ready.

> So do us all a favor
>   and recognize
>   your
>   l i m i t s.

> Step not
>   where you can't
>   s t a n d.

> Because
> the world needs our
>   b r a v e r y
>   so much more
>   than we need
>   your   f e a r f u l
>   love.

WHEN HE TELLS YOU

When he tells you he
"does not understand
what it's like to struggle"
somewhere, somehow, inside,
in the darker corners of the mind
where the sunlight sometimes forgets to shine –
he is lying to you.

When he says he
"really wishes he could understand,"
help you rummage through your rubble,
but instead reminds you that you are different,
distant, an island of pain he has never visited –
he is lying to himself.

When he tells you this,
pay attention to how he
curls his lips into a shield;
Raises his voice to drown out
the hollow echo of his tin armor;
Please, listen for the alarms over
his rust-creaking mechanical smile;
I beg you, press your ear to the floor and
hear the vibrations of what he is really saying:

He is warning you that he cannot, will not face his human.
That he is terrified to stare directly into his
vulnerable, imperfect sun.
That he cannot hold your brave heart without
admitting his own shameful cowardice,
his unsullied hands unfit to be
the keeper of your soul.

Beautiful girl,
when he tells you
you are broken,
Remind him
you are brave,
And that you
would never
prefer the alternative.

STANDING ALONE IN THE DARK

I offered up my poems like sacrifices
And painted him a God

Wished him into a stargazer
And my words,
Comets across his sky

I waited with an almost biblical patience
Standing stock still on the sands of my island
Because surely he would see the red hot firework flares,
Traces from the night my heart burst

But there is so much to be learned from standing alone in the dark

Foremost of which is that
I am grateful he has left me here

Here, in the deepest pit of my despair, I have learned to save myself
I have learned that my poems are not sacrifices,
but great monuments

And not to him
But to the fire in my soul
And to the people who proved that real love
Never leaves

Here, I learned that my poems are comets
And they light up *my* sky
Guiding me home like a North Star that I keep
tucked in my pocket when I sleep at night
And I share them
Spread them out on the table like an atlas for the wanderers,
lost like me
Trying to find their way back to themselves,
Because that's how we all make it out of here alive anyway

So thank god
That I stared down *this* darkness
And sat here on *this* shore
Long enough to see that my poems
Are made for *so much more*
Than his eyes

BRIGHT RED BEATING BALLOON HEART

I have been burned by my ability to romanticize
more times than I can count;
Painted stars into the eyes of those
whose skies were too clouded for constellations.

How could my bright red beating balloon heart
not get carried away on a cool breeze
on warm afternoons,
when sunlight seemed to wash the sidewalks clean
of every step that ever stamped my soul –
only to awake on cold mornings
to fresh boot prints in the snow?

Tell me,
what is the recovering romantic to do?
Stare at blank walls until the paint chips,
revealing arbitrary truths?
Scratch at mirrors,
begging for clarity?

I have done all this and more,
and yet still fail to trust my torpid sense of reason
when the sunlight starts to slip through the blinds.

Perhaps it is time to walk to the river.

Find the sweet spot:
Somewhere between sidestepping the shore
and becoming submerged.

Perhaps it's time to try something new.

HONEST THINGS

I stared into a mirror
and saw a stranger.

It is the most honest thing
I've done all week.

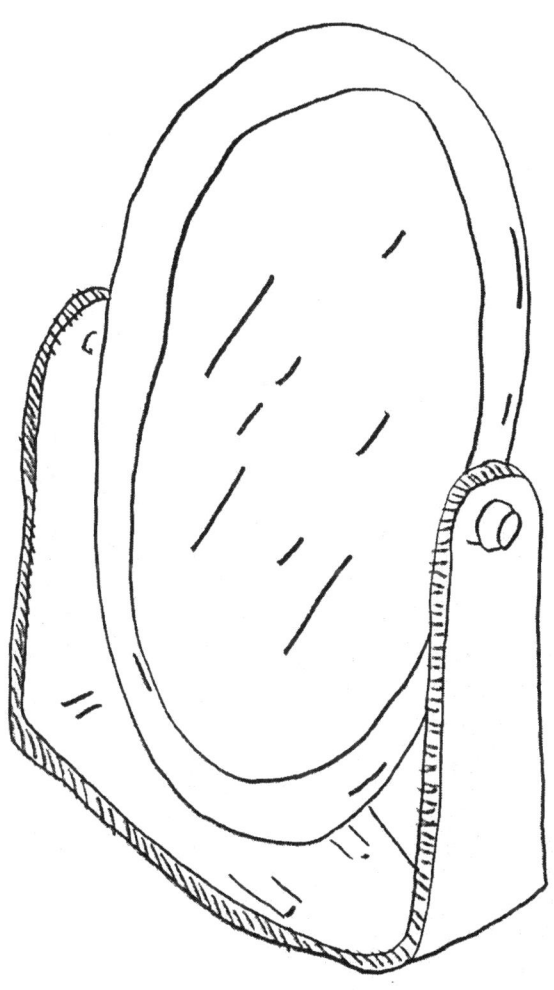

PERHAPS TOMORROW

Some days,
I am small enough to fit inside a paper bag,
crinkled and tossed lightly in a wastebasket
on a street corner.

And some days,
the enormity of my sadness
is enough to eclipse every slice of sunlight,
sending storm cloud shadows over dry pavement in the park.

And while
I hoped
to redeem
this poem
with all the days
that I
am big
and my sadness
small,
the words –
they did not come.

And that is okay.
Because today is not one of those days.

Perhaps tomorrow.

A WOUND THAT'S HEALING

I think
I forgot
how not to write about you.

I think
I forgot
how to write about things
that are not you.

I think
I'll start remembering
to write about those.

- A Wound That's Healing

BRICK

Just as the rain cloud passes

to reveal a golden ceiling,

so

will time pass

and bring forth

your healing.

YOURSELF A WOUND

Imagine yourself a wound;
One massive, open sore,
raw and vulnerable and pained
like a dull ache in a rotted out tooth;
you yearn for healing.

Then, imagine yourself a scar;
open wound turned to scab,
like reverse weathering.
A thing, once sore and sad,
now sealed over with only the suggestion that it once was.

Now, ask yourself:
how?
How does wound become scab become scar?
It is the age-old question of the alchemists,
the transmutation of that bitter,
metallic taste in your mouth
into something golden, something magical
something healed.

TODAY, I AM AN OPEN WOUND

Today,
　　I am an open wound.

All
　　raw nerve ending
and
　　electric ache.

And I cannot decide
　　whether
to be woeful of the
　　pain

or to be grateful
　　to
　　feel
anything at all

11:11

It's 11:11 and I'm wishing I didn't exist.
The truth slides down my bedroom walls like a
thick, murky sludge.
I stick my finger in and it tastes like you,
like failure,
like existential dread.

Fast forward.

It's 11:11 and I'm trying to catch a train,
A train that may or may not exist and could be on any platform.
I don't know where it leads to,
But the sense of panic in my belly says
if I don't catch it,
I'll be stranded.

Fast forward.

It's 11:11 and I think I swallowed a seed.
It's tucked itself quietly into my rib cage
and promises to grow slowly, gently.
Somehow I am simultaneously wishing to
spit it out and
never, ever let it die.

It's 11:11 and suddenly I want to exist again.

ACCEPTANCE

acceptance: it burns
enough of the forest down
to plant life anew

ABOUT THE UGLY

I'm ready to write about the ugly:

Those days when
you were cold water in my warm bath;
how your voice grated harsh upon my ear
like the antithesis of deliverance

Those days when
I was a breadcrumb you dropped along the path;
the one you forgot to retrieve
when you'd found
a new route home
placeholder, saver of space

I'm ready to write about
veiled smiles and full threats –
or maybe it was
full smiles and veiled threats –

I was never sure with you

But I'm ready to write about
Ready to write about you
That other side of you
Those ugly days with you

I'm ready to write about the ugly.

A LOVE NOTE TO MY ARCH-NEMESIS

You
are so beautiful
You, who rubs me the wrong way
You, who rubs my skin raw some days
who gets on my nerves, frayed…

I
am sorry that I
make you about me sometimes.
But you are never about me.
You are always about you.

I
am sorry that I
misplace you; Place you center-
stage in my funhouse mirror mind.
No, you never asked for that.

You
are just existing.

Melissa Felson

UNDERSTAND

I've decided that I'll
n e v e r
u n d e r s t a n d
y o u

but that's okay
because I
u n d e r s t a n d
m e

and that was
my only responsibility
in the
f i r s t
p l a c e

HAMMOCK HARMONY

Remember the time
we laid on that hammock,
you and I?
One of my legs
wrapped around yours,
our arms splayed
lazily above our heads,
twisting our fingers
playfully
through the threads
of the hammock rope…

Remember when we realized
that we could make that hammock sing?
Plucking at the taut strings,
turning vibrations into music –
we laughed at our discovery.

Do you remember our silly joy
at the sudden existence
of our own little symphony?
The way we made memories
out of the smallest of moments,
made melodies
out of the raw material of our hearts…
Remember what power we had?

No matter,
I remember,
As I lay here, legs splayed out
Arms stretched lazily above my head
Learning to take up the spaces you left…

And I am granted a small moment of grace
As I press a finger to that old twine
And realize:
The music is just as beautiful.

PHASES

There is a couple sitting at the table
Where we once tried – and failed –
To reassemble the broken pieces of our love.

They are smiling. They seem new.

Their palms rest
where our fingers once trembled
over coffee cup rims.

Their laughter
lines the curves of our tumulus,
or perhaps I am imagining us out of separate graves again.

In any case,
Maybe it's better this way.

Them, over there.
Us, over here.

In any case,
I hope they make it.

IN DREAMS, I AM FORGIVEN

In dreams, I am floating
above moon-soaked trees
and meandering curlicue rivers;
above every mistake
that once left them
begging for moisture and light,
               d r a i n e d
                          a n d
                                    c r a c k i n g.

In dreams, I press rewind.

                              In dreams,
                    I watch rivers refill,
                              their surging
                                      waters
                    rising up to fill the
                    pit in my stomach.

                    In dreams,
               I watch fallen trees
          rise up like reverse gravity
          lifting with them the weeds
               I've planted in our soil.

In dreams, I am made clean.
In dreams, I am forgiven.

FLOAT AWAY

I fold you, first in half,
then in fourths, then again in thirds.

I rip carefully along your edges.

I move, not angrily,
but with gentle determination
along your creased and riven contours
until you are a small pile of yellowed squares in my palm.

For a moment, I consider you.

Then, release you into open air
lifting my arms with great effort,
a pantomime of exultation,
as you cascade, confetti
    -    I have turned you into celebration.

Humbled, I admire your descent.

Let you fall about me like a fresh snowfall,
until your pieces land
final, on the face of the river.

And with grace, I let you float away.
And with grace, I let you float away.

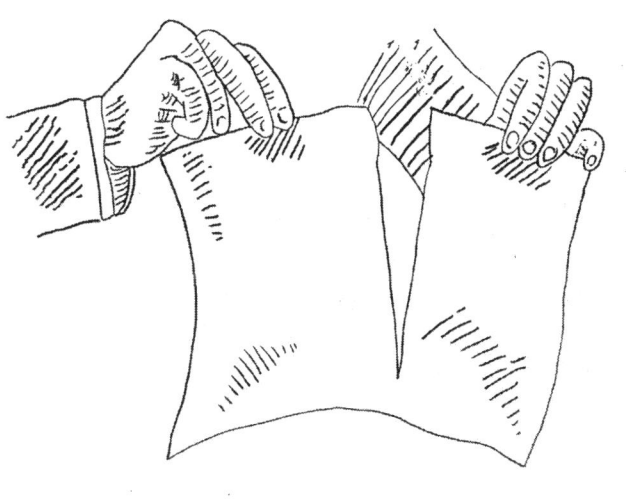

LOTUS

My heart opens like a lotus flower
Thick, thousand-year-old stems rise steadily from the river bottom

Pink bud peeking out above fat floating leaves
My heart is timid
Raised by roots of mud and muck,
It is taken aback by its own slow blooming,
Surprised by its own verdant self-actualization

My Vishnu heart, my heart of mire
Unstained, parts its petals
And gasps at its own great beauty
Not ornamental, but monumental

Learning to take up space
As it spreads itself wide
My lotus heart
Opens
My lotus heart
Blooms

THE WATER'S EDGE

I was the moon and you were the tide
Our dancing, immaculate in the dark shade of night

But as the sun slowly rose
We forgot the ebb and flow

Lost count of the beat,
Started stepping on each other's toes

And while the sight we could have been
If we had stayed, I'll never know

I'm standing at the water's edge
And I'm letting you go

AN ODE TO MY DEAREST GREMLINS
After "Daring Greatly" by Dr. Brene Brown

Dearest Gremlins,

I know you well.
I don't know you well.
I have known you for longer than I can remember.
I am only just meeting you.

You are the incessant voice that whispers to me
When I am most vulnerable
When I am most honest
When I am most real and most alive
Even when I am most joyous, you arrive

You are fear; you are doubt,
Insecurity, sadness, loneliness;
But, most of all, you are fear.

There is so much I could say to you, my dearest gremlins.
The first and foremost of which is:
>   Thank you.
>   (No, I'm not being facetious. I mean this.)

Sweet, well-meaning gremlins,
You only ever wanted to protect me;
When the kids at school called me names,
You taught me to stay away.
When being honest with my mom made her defensive,
You taught me to stay quiet.

You were my armor,
Allowing me to survive battles
When I was too young and naïve
To fight them with weapons.

So thank you, my dearest gremlins,
But
(I know, there's always a but, right?)
There is something else I've got to tell you.

It's been long overdue, but I wasn't quite sure how to say it.

The thing is...
        I don't need you anymore.
        You see, your tactics – hiding out,

Denying the truth, conceding to the enemy –
Were all fine tools
When I was weak and defenseless.

But now, I am a woman.
A woman who has learned
That it's better to fight the battles
Than to run from them.
A woman who has acquired
An armory of weapons
With which she is proficient;
From mindful self-reflection,
To honest conversation,
To leaning on the shoulders of my comrades.

So, you see, you are no longer necessary.

And what's more,
You are no longer welcome.
Your worn out, wary nature
Holds me back from
The vulnerable moments that make me
Human.

Melissa Felson

Your anxiety clouds my joy
And your doubt keeps me small.
And your loneliness?
Your loneliness is the most toxic of all.

So, in sum, I hope I have let you down easily.
Your service, dear gremlins,
has been much appreciated.

But today,
As I should have done
Quite some time ago,

I am showing you the door.

Today, and from today forward,
You will no longer take up residence –

Nor space, nor energy, nor power –
Within my soul.

Respectfully no longer yours,
Me

RIVER RISE

My anxiety
is a house with the doors painted yellow.
(I once read that yellow is an inviting color.)

In each window, there is a potted plant –
enough to please every taste and preference.

When it rains, you can hear her humming
to drown out the sounds of the river rising.

My anxiety

(I.) sits in the parlor with a cup of tea.

(II.) sits in the kitchen with an apron on.

(III.) sits in the bedroom.

(I.) She is trying to write a novel,
    but her hands keep shaking.

(II.) She is trying to cook a meal,
    but her hands keep shaking.

(III.) She is trying to please her husband…

My anxiety
Knows where all the secret hiding places are
And she fills them up like that river
Rising tall,
Hoards it all into crevices
Until the receiving room is spotless.

And when I try to find a nice way to end this,
To remind you
That anxiety is a guest you can disinvite,
My hands begin to shake –

But at least this time,
I won't tidy up my mess.

I let the river rise.

TAPESTRY

My healing is
a tapestry I
wrap myself in
on cold nights

Sewn by those
who have loved me,
Their steady hands,
my courage

Mother to my right
father to my left
all ready grip
and gentle touch

Friends and mentors
stitching bits of
security
that is to say

My healing is
a tapestry I
wrap myself in
on cold nights

And I,
with warmed soul
will ache
with gratitude

An Ode: Brick

MY FATHER IS A GRATITUDE POEM

My father is a gratitude poem
I have been writing my entire life.

He is
calloused hands and soft heart.
Takes his coffee dark and bitter,
but never forgets to slip
that extra spoonful of sugar in my cup.

My father once found me
doubled over on the bedroom floor,
fat wet tears above
my labor-of-love writing journal
that had been ravaged
by an open water bottle in my bag.

My father is
quick thinking and quick feet down the stairs.
He is the stacks of blank notepads
whose pages separated the soggy mess of my words
and he is the sunlight that baked them into legibility again.

Kindness is my father's first language.
He practices giving the shirt off his back
almost as much as he does his guitar,
which is to say
always.

And if Dad Jokes were an Olympic sport
this dad would be the most decorated;
passing down corny jokes
like most parents pass down genes.

I used to complain I didn't get his blue eyes.
Instead, he gave me thick eyebrows
and a knack for losing everything.

But he packaged gifts in boxes reading
Always Tell the Truth
(even the little things)
and Failure is Not an Option
(even when it seems certain).
So I thank him
by reflecting back his honesty
and never giving up.

You see, my father is fixer
of broken eyeglasses and broken hearts.
Drills screws into one
and applies laughter liberally to the other.

He is
I literally wouldn't be me without you and
I can't even stand the thought
of you not being on this Earth…

But
you can't just say this to a man
whose life is built on never bragging.
He'll self-depreciating joke all over your words
and remind you of how great YOU are.

So instead,
you turn him
into a poem
and let it speak
for itself.

FRIENDSHIP BRACELETS

The moment I realized
I had written more poems than I can count
about him and how he broke my heart,
but hadn't written
a single line
about my friends –

My pick-you-up-off-the-floor,
let-you-sob-in-my-passenger-seat,
hate-him-enough-for-the-both-of-us-
when-you-can't-wade-through-the-sadness-
far-enough-to-find-anger
friends –

Was the moment I decided
to finally throw off my chains
and stack each arm to the elbows
with friendship bracelets.

A BALLAD FOR MY FRIENDS

If I could,
I would line my friends up
and name each one of them
like they were seven lifesaving dwarves.

Because
there is so much to be said for Solid.
And Compassionate.
For Loyal, for Real and for Caring.
So much gratitude to be had
for Thoughtful and for Kind.

And if I could,
I would break into song
like they do in the musicals,
because each would get their own ballad:

A ballad of remember the time
I made a home out of your couch?

The time we talked in the car till the sky woke up?

The time you taught me that my broken parts were beautiful?

Or when my manic melted in your give it to me straight?

Remember the time
my phone lit up with "Are you okay?" in the same room as yours?

Or when you broke down each path that led to he doesn't deserve
me?

And I'll never forget
when I was caught in the crash
by your gentle seatbelt arm...

Yes.

A ballad of you are irreplaceable.

A ballad of where would I be without you.

A ballad of thank you thank you thank you
thank you thank you thank you thank you.

WHAT I LEARNED AT CROSSFIT

Burpees suck.

Burpees suck, but not as much as the Assault Bike.

The Assault Bike sucks,
but not as much as never finding out what you're made of.

Finding out what you're made of is not about the mirror.
Turns out, it never was.

Finding out what you're made of is not about CrossFit.
Turns out, that was just the beginning.

Your first competition,
you'll damn near shit your pants.

But you won't.

And the word "Teamwork"
will be etched on your heart
by the most unexpected of hands.

Before you know it,
it will be replaced by "Family."

And when they achieve,
pride will swell in your throat
as if it was your own,

and you'll know what it is
to inhale inspiration.

Grace is found
in the strangest of places
and all it takes
is a willingness to look for it.

Rock bottom
is not actually a bottom,
but a trick floor
you must be brave enough
to fall through.

Handstands aren't a pipe dream
and neither is happiness.

And every damn day,
you can prove yourself wrong.

Every damn day,
you can sail into that familiar storm of fear
and come out the other side without sinking.

Every damn day,
you are a Phoenix.

You will always rise,
bruised but never broken.

SIGNS OF GROWTH

I know I am growing,

because I can no longer

sit comfortably inside my own skin

when I am compelled to act

as anyone other than myself.

WHOLE

When I first met you, I was whole.
A soul with shine in golden seams.
But, slowly, then you took from me
All I had that made me gleam.

Took from me? I handed you!
Tufts of hair, the red of my cheeks,
My diamond eyes, the teeth which formed my smile.
And, in their place, you left me with a hole
Gaping
in the place where my soul had been.

One day I bent
To press a finger there,
Bent until my spine was
Twisted, mangled
Eyes wide
And I, spent
Like a body on loan – returned naught
I screamed with my hand over my mouth,
with my hand over his mouth,
with his hand over my mouth.

And then, all at once, I am someone and no one.
My heart stops, yet beats wildly in my ears.
Words cannot form, while years of articulations rise to the surface.
My spirit has been broken,
And yet it has somehow never been so healed.
It is a time of contradictions;
A time of losing
And of finding.

I wish
With a terrible ferocity, I wish
That I could tell you what I found at the end of this.
I wish I could declare to you:
Here! Here I am! I have found myself
And shall know myself all the days of my life.
But,
Wondrously and painstakingly,
I cannot.

I cannot and I do not and I will not ever know myself whole.
And yet, when I reach to press a finger
Upon the sinews of my soul
I need not bend or break.

And now, the whole world is conspiring to remind me
That those who suppose to love us
Are not supposed to leave us with these glaring, gaping holes
And, no!
They're not supposed to take our holes and make us whole!
Instead, they are supposed to stand beside us, whole
Adoring the shine that fills our soul,
Honoring the part
that comprise our whole.

LOVE LETTERS

I sucked on love letters

like air through a straw.

Shallow sips,

always leaving me breathless.

Today, I write my own love letters.

Oh, how my lungs are bursting.

SUGAR-SUBSTITUTE

People keep telling me
I look amazing.
They beg:
tell us your secret.
what have you been doing?

I tell them:
I've made some changes to my diet.

I've stopped putting
external validation
in my morning coffee.

(sugar-substitute, highly processed
packaged sweetener
made of
artificial
Instagram likes and
bending over backwards like
acrobatics for attention;
blending myself into
you for approval
like stirring in your
favorite brand of
soy milk even though
soy makes me sick.)

I tell them
I opt for the real thing these days.
Organic
connection and
act natural, which is to say:
Don't act.
Be.

And, sure, it's hard to kick the habit and
I'm not perfect at it, but –
I tell them –
Life is much sweeter this way.

IN A KAYAK ON A THURSDAY

Not too long ago
Not so far from here
I was crouched in a bathroom crying
at a party,
unbeknownst to the many people
on the other side of the door,
and for no reason
other than
I hurt –
a deep, knowing hurt
that pierced my belly
and, on occasion,
rose into my throat
but was never permitted
to quite reach my eyes.

Today,
I am sitting in a kayak
on a Thursday
by myself.

In a kayak that I bought,
In a kayak that I learned how to transport,
In a lake that I found.

But what is most profound
is that I am in a kayak
with a happiness that I sought,
taught myself to find,
and fight for every day of my life.

Today,
I know what it is
for my smile to reach my eyes
and to be the one
who put it there.

CLAY

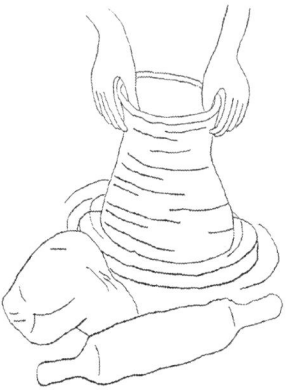

I am hardened still,

but the way you soften me

is such a beautiful thing.

WHAT LIST SHOULD I TURN INTO POETRY?

After Liz Mercedes - @liz.mercedes_poetry

1. items crossed off of my childhood bucket list
2. metaphors I've used to write about my mother

3. a catalog of therapy sessions that stitched me back together
4. all the men that I magicked from mole hills into mountains

5. my friends and fifteen ways
   that each of them have saved me
6. five secrets that only my dog knows

7. nights I spent wishing myself into stardust
8. days I spent living like sunshine

9. ten poets that changed my life forever
10. three nightmares I'll probably never get over

11. fifty reasons why I am my own best friend
    and all of the years it took to write them

WHAT I HAVE LEARNED

here's what I have learned:

you have not met yourself
until you have met yourself in free fall

trap door blown out below you
heart taking up residence in your throat

and I will tell you this:

you will not enjoy dropping weightless
into the abyss

but it is the only way
you will ever learn to fly

I WEEP

I weep
a bouquet of flowers
into my own hands

first, the pruning
ruthless removal
cut and pull
of gentle bud and root
from solid ground
surgical, sacred practice

and then, the watering
essential mourning
of life and lifeless
petals tumbling
satin tears
falling
through splayed fingers
mixing
into the soil of my soul
a powerful nourishing

yes,
I weep
a bouquet of flowers
into my own hands
so that I
may grow

THE INEVITABLE PHYSICS OF LIGHT

Sometimes your light will dim.
It is inevitable.
Physics, really.

And so,
it is your charge
to love yourself
so fiercely
and deeply
and defiantly
that you are tirelessly committed
to keeping your light burning.

You must do this for you, entirely,
and no other soul can do it for you.

I AM IN LOVE WITH IRONY

I am in love with irony.

With how
drawing lines in the sand
with the people we love
is like tracing pointed arrows
at where they can love us best.

With how
sitting cross-legged
in the center of our sadness,
studying a cross-section of our struggle,
is like the exhale of fumes
and the inhale of peace.

With how,
if you take one hand off the handlebar
and place it squarely upon your chest,
you will be steered in the direction of your wisest heart
as if rearranging TV antennas at just the right angles.

Oh yes, I am in love with irony;
In love with letting go to leave my hands free for fullness,
In love with shedding armor to finally know my own strength,
In love with finding joy on the flipside of the coin of pain.

HEAVY HURT

oh, to feel that heavy hurt
that holy strain

a faint crescendo of throbbing
that spreads, wildfire
across my sinewy shoulders
propelling me as I
push
push
push
pumping my arms like a heartbeat

to drink it in –
that sacred sting
of salt like
sugar to my eyes,
back bared
welcoming
the lashes of the sun

to feel each ripple,
each blessed bead of sweat –
to relish in that heady burn,
thin layer of tears, blinked
back and
push
push
push

that,
oh, that
is the stuff of life

SOMETIMES YOU WILL BE MORE VILLAIN THAN HERO

I have always tread so lightly;
tiptoed across the pages of other people's lives,
so as not to wrinkle them with my weight.

I have been more
carefully choreographed dance than character

for fear of misstepping
into the role of somebody else's villain.

But plot twists and story arcs
and a sheer lack of happy endings
have taught me a few lessons:

Sometimes you will be more villain than hero.
And, sometimes, they won't remember you well.

And when you exhale,
and you finally let the vapor of your honesty
free from the prison of your fear,

and when it mixes with the hot cooker pressure
of your building self-respect,
you will crease a couple of pages.

You will step heavier.

And you should.

TINDER BOX

I am a tinder box
a cinderblock, a dying flame
at once, a bout of something sad
and something quite and sane

I am a four course meal
that never touched more than a porcelain plate
one breath, a valiant steed
and next inhale
a filly, lame

how I breach these walls,
diffuse and all but miracle
I do not know, but straddle still
ethereal

how I span these spaces
light but somehow heavy full
I do not know, but matter still
immaterial

TOUCH TREE
after "Untamed" by Glennon Doyle Melton

A few summers ago, when I was still living with my parents, I found
myself splayed out on the hammock in our backyard.

I remember myself in that moment:
Breathing deeply, gazing up at the intricate network of branches and
the full green leaves above my head, considering…

In a few months, those leaves will be brown.

In a few more months, those branches will be bare.
And those leaves will be all crunch and fodder on the ground.

And next summer,
when new leaves have arrived to take their place, where will I be?
Will I still live here, at home, with my parents?
What will my life be like then?

And what about many years from now?
When I pause to take a breath in my good, old, trusty hammock –
How much will have changed?
How much will have remained?

I am reading a book by Glennon Doyle.
In it, she speaks of a "Touch Tree."

She explains that, when a person is lost in the woods,
a touch tree is "one recognizable, strong, large tree
that becomes the lost one's home base."

She talks of how we must each become our own touch trees:
Perpetually returning to ourselves
whenever we feel lost.

I am reading this on my hammock, three years later.

In that time, I have left home,
had my heart broken and returned home.

I have planted the seeds of new friendships
and tilled the soil to revitalize old ones.

I have had several nephews born into this world.
I have had several friends leave it.

And still, I lay here.

Still, gazing up at the very same pattern
of sturdy, angled branches and lush, green leaves.

Still, breathing deeply.

Except this time, I understand.

This time, I know that I don't need to worry.

That no matter what changes...
No matter what pain, heartache,
fear or despair arrive at my doorstep...
no matter what the address of that doorstep is...

I will always have my Touch Tree.

INHERITANCE

I refuse to feel shame
For my fear and insecurity
Passed down to me by my mother
And her mothers before her

I will wear it like a badge
For it has stripped each of us raw,
Opened us up like budding roses

Striped us with war paint and wisdom
Taught us to rise against the darkest tides
Within ourselves

Try as you will
You cannot make me apologize
For carrying, like redemption,
The very weapons that once wounded me

This is my sacred alchemy
This is my brand of bravery
The likes of which you will never know

DON'T STARVE THE MOTHER WOUND

When you locate the core
emotion,
when you identify the source
trauma,
you may be tempted to
cut
the umbilical ties as a way to
escape
the
pain.

Instead,
poke around.
Inhale
her origins, trace her
tendrils
all the way back to the
center
and let her, and all of the
other
mother wounds before her,
heal
on
a

counter
by an open window
where you, and your mother,
and her mother have all stood,
where your daughter
will one day stand,
nurtured
and
free.

THE BRAVEST WOMEN I KNOW

The most courageous women I know

are the ones who were brave enough

to continue loving themselves

after the world told them

they shouldn't.

UNFOLD YOUR TONGUE

Unfold your tongue;
Untwist its sharp edges into
Origami backwards
Like a Chinese staircase
Undone by fervent fingers; fold

Your truth into a homemade apple pie
Bake it at 375 and serve it piping
With a dollop of your favorite vanilla ice cream
Steaming

Scream all you want
While you're baking
Let the pain seep into the air pockets
And those things you've kept quiet
Riot within the rising dough

I promise
I'll eat it anyway

HER WORDS

There are the words I'm too afraid to say
for fear of you not liking me,

The words that crouch quietly inside me
because well… who likes fighting?

These are the thoughts and opinions and conclusions
that might not bode nicely,

But I'll be damned if they're not well thought out,
articulate and expressed concisely.

This is the girl who was too afraid to be a woman
too afraid of her own power,
because power means sticking it to them.

This is the woman who is still afraid
but learning her own courage every day;

Earning her stripes, the stripes on her uniform
that she wears as she heads to war

each morning, after looking in the mirror,
reminding that girl that she matters -

Her words, her opinions, they matter.

And what's more, people are listening.
With baited breath, you, you are listening.
And if she chose, out of fear, not to speak
You would not hear her.
You would not know her.

But she, she rises.
Out of the ashes of the people
who told her she did not matter,
That she could not possibly speak
and be heard with clarity.

Her voice, it rises.

And these, these are her words.

A LETTER TO MYSELF AS A FIFTY-FIVE-YEAR OLD SINGLE
WOMAN

Dear me,
Dear beautiful, capable, badass me,

I see you.
One man show worthy of a million viewers and needing none.
World an oyster; You, a pearl
that refuses to be set in the collar of any man's charm.

I see you out there.
Singing and writing and teaching
and dancing your daring solo dance across the Earth
reminding the world that dancers do not require partners in order to
be worthy of the stage.

I see you,
and my eyes – that is, your eyes
are the only eyes that matter.

And my heart – that is, your heart
is no smaller
no weaker
loves no less than the heart that is occupied.

Do not be preoccupied
with the weight of expectations
thrown carelessly on your shoulders.
It is not your weight to bear.

You are fire and flame.
Not simply rib,
but head and heart and hips
and lips whose cause is not to kiss
but to lift the spirits of those you love.

Love is a four letter word.
Not an accolade, but an action word.
A verb that swerves in so many directions,
that cannot be defined
by the presence or absence of a partner.
You cannot be defined by the presence or absence of a partner

You are love.
And I see you.
The world sees you.

AN UNLEARNING

I used to think I needed to be loved and admired to be enough.

When I was seven, I learned
that looking out for my brother meant that my grandparents
would point out "what a good big sister I am."

When I was nine, I learned
that if I got up in the middle of the night and cleaned the house,
it would make my mom happy and she would
tell me how much she loves me.

When I was eleven, I learned
that when a boy tells you to kiss him and
you hesitate, he puts you in a headlock, and when you kiss said boy,
it feels warm and fuzzy like I love you does.

When I was thirteen, I learned
there was more warm and fuzzy where that came from –
in a sixteen-year-old boy's bedroom when his parents weren't home
and
that is when I first learned
to search for I love you's in a rough embrace.
When I was nineteen, I learned
that it's easier to spend four years with constant I love you's, even
when they don't quite reach your heart, because
it's safer than letting it go and the risk of never getting it back.

Then, when I was twenty-one,
and warm fuzzy feelings from boys who took more than they gave
had left me empty,
I began to learn that the most important I love you's
don't come from grandmas or moms or boys whose lips make you
feel on fire.

And when I was twenty-three,
I said I love you to myself and, for the first time, I meant it.
I've said it every day since.

Tomorrow, I will be twenty-four.
What will I learn next?

I USED TO

I used to stoke my fire
with someone else's heat.

But today, I was ignited
by my own relentless passion.

I used to wear the lenses
of others to color my image.

But today, I pass a mirror
and needed no reflection to know me.

I used to fill my moments
with the salve of people's presence.

But today I chose my solitude
and felt my body healing.

I used to be inflated
by the breath another gave me.

But today, I inhaled deeply
and felt it fill my soul.

INTO THE MINEFIELDS

Into the minefields
we warriors go
to face our pain
and claim our souls

and there,
as soldiers of our hearts,
become whole.

SUCH FRAGILE PLACES FOR STRENGTH

I have seen great strength
packaged in such fragile boxes

trembling lips trying to form words in an attempt to read

"C-
c-c-a,
c-c-ca-at."

hands like butterfly wings
carrying her sister's will

heavy
        like a
                tomb

the wet of his cheeks
of his unblinked back tears
even though his dad said to

take it
        like a
                man

and all I can do
is watch in wonder;

such dark places for light
such ugly places for beauty
such fragile places for strength

BETTER

I sat inside a room
and promised myself
I wouldn't come out
until I was "better."

You see,
no one taught me
that better
is not a chalked line in the dirt,
that there is no
bronzed medal with gilded rim
reading:
Better. Fit for consumption.

I stared down a mirror
so long
that my lips became my eyes
and my eyes became
huge craters
I couldn't climb out of.

But I didn't care for climbing anyhow.
Instead,
I became a master excavator.

Proud,
albeit lonely.

Tools in hand,
refusing hands of rescue
reaching out from the rim.

"I'm fine. Really, I'm fine."

"She was,
in fact,
not fine,"
reads the narrator.

These days I've learned
that dogs see in black and white,
but I am not a dog.
I am human.

I am human,
so I err.
I am human,
so I am flawed.

I am human,
so no amount of
excavation,
recreation,
reflection
or divine inspiration
will deem me "better."

But
I am human,
so I am enough

HOPE

Somewhere between fear and naiveté,
There is a warm, golden pool of light
Wherein we can enjoy the cool waters
Without the danger of drowning.
It is called:
Hope.

YEAR OF UNTANGLING

To my year of tangled yarn,
Year of twisted bike chain at the park,
Year of melted chocolate on my favorite red sweater,
Year after chocolate feast on the couch with my new lover.

To my banged and bruised year,
My tissues used year –
Piled high against the wall
like a monument of surrender.

Surrender
is what I begged for –
Escape
from you, year.

Year of "When it rains it pours,"
"When one door closes, another one opens."
Silver linings on rain clouds filled like bile in my mouth.
I spit them out and swallowed gulps of air to keep breathing,
Seething, at you, year.

I'd never been so glad to see December.

It's November.

The pile of tissues have made their way to the wastebasket.

My red sweater, freshly cleaned,
brings out the copper in my concentrated eyes.

Hapless strings of multicolored yarn
stretch comfortably on my bedroom floor.
Each untangled arm reaches back
to a small sphere in my lap.

I am humming.

I don't realize I am humming,
but as I pull each inch of contorted mess into neat lines,
I am content.

Tangled yarn year, twisted chains year
Year of nearly ruined sweaters,
I promise to remember you better.
Grant you your honor due:

Year of patience, year of cleansing,
Year of untangling

A MILLION ENDINGS

I am a mystery
even to
myself

Like looking through
frosted glass
I begin
to second guess

I am a performer
with a choice:
Play to soothe
the whining critics
or a writhing inner voice

I am a novel
half-read on the kitchen table,
a million endings
suspended in thick air

Melissa Felson is a 28-year-old poet from Long Island, New York. Her work has been featured in Nassau Voices in Verse, Eve Poetry Literary Magazine, Poetry in the Time of Coronavirus, Remington Review Online Literary Journal and in A.B.Baird's recent anthology "My Still Waters." Melissa is a special education teacher and aspiring BCBA, and can often be found playing ukulele and throwing 'Writing Celebrations' in her classroom. In her free time, she loves to: perform poetry and music at open mics; read in her hammock or on her kayak; and explore new places – always with an iced coffee in hand.

If you have enjoyed this work by Melissa Felson, you can read more on Instagram at @intotheminefields.

Steven Felson is a 27 year old young man living in Massapequa, New York. He is diagnosed with ASD and began expressing himself through art at very early age. Steven has presented his art in pop-up exhibits at the Queens Museum of Art and has had his work featured on greeting cards and postcards. He enjoys drawing movie posters, going to the movie theater and going out to eat with his family.

Printed in Great Britain
by Amazon